Secrets of the U.S. Tax Code

In 10 Easy Segments

By Anonymous

Copyright 2017
by the Maine Republic Free State

This information is offered for educational purposes only; not to be taken as legal advice.

All Rights Reserved
Parts of this book may be reproduced subject to due and specific acknowledgment of their source.

from the
Maine Republic Email Alert
3 Linnell Circle
Brunswick, Maine 04011

www.mainerepublicemailalert.com

CONTENTS

SECRETS OF THE U.S. TAX CODE
— in 10 Easy Segments —

1. **Segment 1 – Introduction** ---------------------------------- 5
2. **Segment 2 – What About the Sixteenth Amendment?** -- 10
3. **Segment 3 – Those Pesky Terms of Art** --------------- 14
4. **Segment 4 – How You Volunteered** --------------------- 17
5. **Segment 5 – Falling Into the IRS Trap!** -------------- 21
6. **Segment 6– Troubles with W-4 and W-9** ------------- 25
7. **Segment 7– So What Do You Do Now?** --------------- 29
8. **Segment 8—Why It's Important** ------------------------ 32
9. **Segment 9 – A Question about Information Returns** -- 36
10. **Segment X – What About Capital Gains?** --------- 39
11. **A Caveat:** --- 43

FOOD FOR THOUGHT

For the past 104 years of its existence, the U.S. Internal Revenue Code has been ridiculed, feared, and despised virtually by everyone. And why not? As presented by the Internal Revenue Service, the Code appears to be illogical, inconsistent, and incomprehensible. It defies practically the entire Bill of Rights– by requiring citizens to testify against themselves, by allowing searches and seizures without warrants, by levying fines and penalties without trials, and by imposing a tax on our basic right to earn a living. As presented by the IRS, the IRC appears to turn everything we all thought we had learned in grade-school English and Civics on its head.

SECRETS OF THE U.S. TAX CODE
— in 10 Easy Segments —

Segment 1 - Introduction

Will your eyes glaze over and will you run for the exit if I broach the subject of the income tax? You will if you're like most folks in the U.S.A.

Like so many others, you may consider the income tax to be the most "little-to-be-done-about" subject that one might wish to write about. You might hate paying the tax, you might wish you could get away from paying it, but you're convinced you *must* pay it because "that's just the way it is." You are also likely to be scared to death of the IRS, but you're a good citizen, essentially, and you may even believe you've got a patriotic duty to "pay your fair share."

However, more and more Americans are discovering that the federal government has been withholding the truth about the income tax, as with so many of its other operations. The tax is actually a benign but grossly misunderstood **excise tax** affecting only a small percentage of the American public.

It's simply not in the government's interest to tell you the facts about the tax. They prefer that the public remains deaf, dumb, and scared as hell, about it — probably as you likely are right now. Their attitude is that it's not their job to educate you about the tax. Just shut up and pay it.

I hope you'll hear me out here. You won't read this or hear

it from your "tax adviser," even if you ask him/her, point blank. That person is as much in the dark as you are!

It is this widespread ignorance of basic tax law that leads to you getting victimized every payday, first by the system, then by your equally uninformed boss at work, and his CPA, and —unfortunately— by the Internal Revenue Service itself, which is happy to take your money even when you owe them nothing.

But to be fair, the IRS annually deals with hundreds of scams and nutty ideas about how to avoid or escape paying the tax. You might consider what I'm writing here to be in that same category: a scheme, or some crackpot idea. Nevertheless, I urge you to read on here, because what I'm about to reveal to you is the absolute proven truth, as I'll detail to you. Even the IRS, albeit with some cajoling, admits it to be the truth!

Little by little, mostly by word of mouths like mine— person to person— the facts are being revealed, despite the best efforts of the IRS to "keep a lid" on it. Many thousands have learned these facts and, quite legitimately, have freed themselves from paying the tax.

We must start at the beginning with the United States Constitution, the basic law of the land. It all begins here. If you're like most people, you've likely never *seen* a copy of the Constitution, let alone read it. It's not long and it's not complicated. Over the years, politicians and courts have punched it into a shape more to their liking, but, even so, it remains the fundamental law of the land. There is no

United States of America without the Constitution.

All Federal and State Laws must be seen and read in the light of the Constitution and its 27 Amendments.

"The Bill of Rights" is comprised of the first ten Amendments of the Constitution. In my opinion, <u>everything that is wrong with the U.S.A. today can be traced to politicians and jurists either ignoring the Constitution entirely, or "interpreting" its resolutions to suit their various political or economic fancies</u>.

Over the years, the people have been led to think that the Sixteenth Amendment authorized the income tax, and that the tax covers any and all income except for that specifically exempted. This is simply not true, but the IRS doesn't object that most people believe it. It suits their purpose to keep the people both ignorant and scared.

So here's the beginning of what you don't know:

The Sixteenth Amendment did not really amend the Constitution at all! The Constitution plainly established that there are only two types of federal taxes permitted in the U.S.A. One is a capitation tax (per head) or a <u>direct tax— provided</u> that such a tax is laid upon each of the 50 States according to the proportion of their total population. This is called "apportionment."

The other type of permitted tax is an <u>indirect tax</u>, in the form of **duties**, **imposts** and **excises**, provided that they are uniform in nature.

We know that the federal income tax is not a direct tax because it is not apportioned. It is in fact an excise tax— which means that it is based on privileged activity— it is a piece of the action levy that stems from a connection to the federal government in a way that produces a monetary benefit. In other words, it is NOT all-pervasive. It does NOT cover "all that comes in."

> **"The income tax is, therefore, <u>not</u> a tax on income as such. It is an excise tax with respect to certain activities and privileges, which is measured by reference to the income which they produce. The income is not the subject of the tax: it is the basis for determining the amount of tax."** — F. Morse Hubbard, Treasury Department legislative draftsman, House Congressional Record, March 27th 1943, page 2580.

Now, think of the tax you are paying on your income at work. Are you, or is the place where you work, connected by some privilege or activity to the federal government? If not, then why are you paying an income tax?

The reason you pay the tax —let's face it— is because you probably volunteered to pay it! Do you remember volunteering to pay it? No?

Well, you did. When you first went to work, you filled out **"enrollment" forms**. You didn't know it at the time, but in completing and signing those forms, you **enrolled yourself** to pay the **excise tax** on your personal earnings.

Your boss too has been led to believe that he must have you complete the paperwork. So that's what you did in a very routine way. That was not because you are dumb, but because you and he didn't know any better.

This <u>enrollment procedure</u> has become so ingrained, so unthinkingly done, that it has become routine and all-pervasive. "Everybody does it." However, it wasn't always this way. Back before World War II hardly anyone paid the <u>excise tax</u> on earnings. There were no <u>enrollment forms</u>.

I won't go into the why and how of all that just yet. First, you need to digest the fact that all of the talk about <u>taxing the rich and paying your fair share</u>, meaningless federal budgets, raising or lowering marginal tax rates, and all the rest of the political poop, is merely smoke screen. You can choose to believe it or not. But the <u>legal fact of the matter</u> is that IF the enterprise that hired you —or you yourself if you work for yourself!— has no connection to the federal government in some <u>privileged way</u>, and if no other of your earnings have any connection to the federal government, then you are <u>not obligated by law</u> to pay the tax, <u>no matter how much you are earning</u>!

There are no tax brackets to be applied IF your income is NOT of the type to be <u>taxable</u> in the first place.

The basic law of the land holds your <u>private property</u> as sacrosanct, and the most important property right you have is to determine for yourself who you are, and what you are not. This encompasses <u>the right to sell your labor in order to make a living</u>. No one can tax you for doing that. This is because <u>you own yourself</u> and have an <u>unabridged right</u> to enter or not enter into a contract.

If you were taxed on your <u>right of free speech</u> would you object? Of course you would and rightly so. But what about being taxed by **"the system"** on your <u>right to make a living</u>?

> **"The individual**, unlike **the corporation**, cannot be taxed for the mere privilege of existing. **The corporation** is an artificial entity which owes its existence and charter powers to the state; but the <u>individuals' rights</u> to live and own property <u>are natural rights</u> for the enjoyment of which an excise cannot be imposed." — **Redfield v. Fisher, 292 P. 813, 135 OP. 180, 294, P. 461, 73 A.L.R. 721 (1931)**

Segment 2 – What About the Sixteenth Amendment?

You say, look here Mr. Smarty Pants, the Sixteenth Amendment says plainly that

> **"The Congress shall have power to lay and collect taxes on incomes, from whatever source derived, without apportionment among the several States, and without regard to any census or enumeration."**

That certainly <u>seems</u> to state very clearly that the Sixteenth is the legal source of the income tax. But if that's true, then why is it that the very first income tax in America was levied in 1862 by the Lincoln administration, 51 years before the Sixteenth Amendment came into being? That first income tax was not declared unconstitutional. No one found legal fault with it because it was recognized in its day as an excise tax that relatively few people had to deal with. In fact, parts of it are still on the books, while other segments have been reworded. It is still the same excise tax it was in Lincoln's time. The basics of it have not changed one bit.

To get it all into historical perspective, you need to know that in 1895, due to a Supreme Court case resulting from the revival of the income tax in 1894, the court ruled that the earnings from a certain private property could not be taxed because doing so would be tantamount to a property tax— a direct tax which is prohibited by the Constitution unless it is apportioned. Whereupon the court threw out the entire 1894 law. It was ruled unconstitutional.

Because this 1895 Supreme Court decision served to shield the private profits of mostly wealthy exploiters of public resources from the tax, popular sentiment urged Congress to amend the Constitution to overrule the decision. That resulted the Sixteenth Amendment in 1913. Three years later, the excise tax connected to some incomes was re-activated as an addendum to a bill that lowered the duties on imports.

A man named Brushaber didn't like the way things were going so he sued to prevent paying the tax. The lawsuit [*Brushaber v. Union Pacific Railroad*] reached the Supreme

Court in 1916. Their <u>unanimous</u> ruling declared that the Sixteenth Amendment hadn't changed anything fundamental about taxation at all. <u>Direct taxation without apportionment is still forbidden</u>. The work of the amendment — what it does accomplish —is to <u>correct</u> the basic error made by the 1895 court, that the <u>source</u> of earnings is germane to their taxability.

Several other Supreme Court rulings have since confirmed *Brushaber* so it is well-established law. Treasury Ruling No. 2303 states it very succinctly:

> **"The provisions of the Sixteenth Amendment conferred no new power of taxation but simply prohibited the complete and plenary power of income taxation possessed by Congress from the beginning from being taken out of the category of indirect taxation to which it inherently belonged."**

So, let's get beyond the Sixteenth Amendment. It's of little relevance to our main discussion here; namely, that <u>the federal income tax attaches only to earnings that have some connection to the federal government</u>. That is what an excise tax is.

Here's an <u>apt analogy</u> about it: if you open a lemonade stand on a corner of land owned or controlled by the feds, the profits you make can be taxed by the feds, because they are entitled to a piece of your "action." But if you open the same lemonade stand on <u>private property</u> directly across the street, the feds have no claim on your profits regardless of how much money you might take in.

"The income tax is, therefore, not a tax on income as such. It is an excise tax with respect to certain activities and privileges which is measured by reference to the income which they produce. The income is not the subject of the tax: it is the basis for determining the amount of tax." **(F. Morse Hubbard, Treasury Department legislative draftsman, House Congressional Record, March 27th 1943, page 2580)**

Are you getting a clearer picture now?

The Constitution is your friend. It keeps the government off your back —or at least it's purpose is to do that. When you are ignorant of its provisions, you allow yourself to be swept into the incorrect conventional practices now controlling income tax procedure, as well as the adventurism and social theories of political wing-nuts in Congress. You unknowingly cooperate with the robbery of your earnings, and your loss of freedom to retain and control your personal properties and earnings.

How does this make you feel?

(Note: Almost all State income taxes are based on the Federal income tax. If you do not have federally taxable income, then you do not have State taxable income either— no matter how they slice and dice it. There are very few exceptions —those in States which have not based their tax on income on the federal model.)

Segment 3 – Those Pesky Terms of Art

If some crook robbed you of your money at gun point, no doubt you would call the cops and raise hell. Strangely, however, when Uncle Sam does the robbing, *even when you know that he's a crook,* your all-too-typical reaction is that you don't want to anger the IRS or your boss by standing up for yourself. Better to pay "your fair share" like a good little citizen.

All that can be said to this is, if you don't do anything to stop the thievery through the simple expedient of <u>obeying the law</u>, you really are a sad sack, are you not? You may as well be in a Prinson labor camp!

I want to say something else here—concerning the notion that if you're one of the 49% who already do not, for one reason or another, pay any federal income tax (except for surtaxes known as Social Security and Medicare) then you are a rat-fink crook who should be ashamed of yourself. That's an absolutely crazy notion. Why pay a tax —any tax— when there is no lawful obligation to pay it?

The federal income tax is perfectly constitutional—let's get that straight right away from the start. If you have <u>taxable income</u>, you must report it and pay whatever tax on it is due.

But, do you have <u>taxable income</u>? This is the central question to be answered.

So I'm going to tell you the secret that is unknown to

millions of Americans just like you. How the government operates to have you <u>volunteer your earnings</u> as the type of income affected by the income <u>excise tax</u>.

The feds do this by remaining totally silent about the tax code's plentiful use of **"terms of art."** So-called "tax experts" in the income tax industry aren't told either, more about them later. So it becomes a matter of the "blind leading the blind".

A **"term of art"** is a legal term defined in the law itself. Such terms must be understood in their <u>legal sense</u> —not according to their <u>dictionary</u> meaning. Here are some examples of income tax <u>terms of art</u>: **"employee"**, **"employer"**, **"wages"**, **"United States"**, **"State"**, **"Taxpayer"**, **"trade or business"**, **"U.S. Person"**, **"includes/including"**, and more. These seem to be ordinary words, but each of these words has a <u>special meaning</u> provided within the tax code itself. They become <u>legal Terms of Art</u>.

You may think that you are an "employee" working for an "employer" and being paid "wages" but in the context of tax law, most probably you are not. If you or the company you work for has no connection to the federal government, then the feds have no legal right to treat your earnings as "wages" subject to the tax — <u>unless you volunteer yourself into their grasp</u>. And that's exactly what you've done.

Another example: If you are one who works for himself, then the legal definition of **"trade or business"** comes actively into play. Item 26 of Section 7701 defines this term as the **"conduct of the affairs of a public office"**.

A public office is like your lemonade stand on government property. It's the connection to the federal government. Without that connection, no <u>excise tax</u> applies.

Where do you find these legal definitions? One particular section of the tax code is entirely devoted to a bunch of these legal definitions [26 USC, Section 7701(a)]. Others are sprinkled about here and there within the tax "code." Certain of these terms of art are repeated often throughout the code, and you simply have to know them, because, as you've often heard, "ignorance of the law is no excuse". To complicate things still more, the definition of one term quite often contains other <u>terms</u> which also must be looked up in order to arrive at a full legal meaning.

Anyone with an Internet connection can now locate these things for himself. Once you see how the game is played, then all else falls into place. The picture then becomes clear: You are being hoodwinked, and you can stop this foolishness.

Isn't it worthwhile, for you to learn how to stop paying taxes you don't owe?

The income tax system siphons billions of dollars into government coffers each year, precisely because the public is kept ignorant of these terms of art. It amounts to <u>artful thievery</u> —in the same way that a pickpocket takes your wallet without you knowing it. Except that the pickpocket in this case keeps right on doing it to you every payday.

Segment 4 – How You Volunteered

So, how did you <u>volunteer yourself</u> into paying an excise tax on your innate God given right to make a living?

When virtually everyone has been vacuumed into the system, there is little chance that you would consider yourself to be different from every one else. It becomes routine, punctuated by news stories of this or that harebrained tax protester being jailed—just in case you get any smart ideas. Fortunately, it's not a case of once in, always in. Each year's earnings are distinct from another year's earnings. Situations can and do change.

One of the surprising basic facts to become aware of is that the entire tax code applies <u>only</u> to **"taxpayers."** This is another legal term, defined as **"any person"** who is subject to any internal revenue tax.

If there were no particular importance to it, why does the **"taxpayer"** term even exist? Why is a distinction in the code needed at all? But since it is clear to you by now (or should be) that the tax on income is an <u>excise tax</u>, then it stands to reason as well that it does not apply to everybody.

If you are not such a **"taxpayer"** then you are not subject to <u>the tax code</u>. Nevertheless, you are given forms to complete that are designed for use only by **"taxpayers"**.

The feds <u>presume</u> and <u>assume</u> that you are aware of that fact. They don't regard it as their responsibility to tell you.

So when you unthinkingly filled out a form designed for **"employees,"** you tacitly agreed that you are an **"employee"** working for an **"employer"** and being paid **"wages."** You are taken at your word because you enrolled! The IRS attitude as a result becomes: "Pay up and shut up or we'll come and do all kinds of nasty things to you."

Before you begin working for some enterprise, you are routinely given <u>enrollment forms</u> to complete. The two most noteworthy of them are IRS forms titled <u>"W-4"</u> and <u>"W-9"</u>. Both are designed only for **"taxpayer"** use and include <u>contractual terms</u>. But there is no indication about those terms anywhere on those forms. There is no highlighting of the terms, no underlining, no italics, no footnotes. They're just there. Without a second thought, you filled out the forms and sign them under penalty of perjury. And that is the moment you <u>volunteered yourself</u> into the tax system —right up to your eyeballs.

After you sign them, they are operational and in effect. To escape their grasp, you must take steps to <u>unwind</u> or <u>cancel them</u> and <u>withdraw</u> from them. That's often hard to do requiring the cooperation of the company you work for. Once your boss also understands that he too has been hornswaggled, the pathway out of the system's grasp opens to you. You don't complete any forms (not needed), there is no withholding of funds from your pay (not needed), and no informational returns to IRS (also not needed).

If your position with your boss is that he won't hear of making any changes, then your alternative is to counteract the sworn information reports he sends to IRS each

January. There is not room in this brief report to suggest methods or ways to do that. However, that information is available from other sources at your request.

Obviously, when you filled out your work forms you didn't know what you were doing to yourself.

You didn't spend any time delving through the tax statutes. Who does that, after all? You simply take someone's word for it that "it's necessary" or "the law requires it." But no one tells you about those terms of art. This is probably the first you have heard about them.

Here's another surprise: Among the 50 "Titles" referring to all of the laws of the United States, only half of them have been passed into law by the Congress and signed by the President. Title 26, the one that includes the income tax, is among the titles that have never been passed into law.

Title 26 contains a rewriting, a codification, of the "Statutes at Large" each of which was passed into law by Congress. Each and every word of the Statutes at Large has marked significance that may not be changed by anyone.

The codification is an attempt to re-order the Statutes into more readable form. They are supposedly then easier to read and understand. However, the revamped writings lose their prime legal status and must be considered at best, only an important clue as to the underlying laws. Further "clarifications" or "amplifications" are attempted by the Secretary of the Treasury in the form of regulations relating to some sections of the IRC. However, it is a principle of law that both the tax code and Treasury regulations are always subordinate to the <u>Statutes at Large</u>.

There have been <u>four major rewrites</u> of the code over the years, supposedly to simplify its language, but in fact <u>code sections have become ever more verbose</u>. None of the re-writes has changed the basics of the income tax: it remains an <u>excise tax</u> on privileged earnings.

The tax code has millions of words in it. It's a hodge-podge of words and terms and cross-references in no particular order. How on earth is anyone supposed to make heads or tails of it?

If it weren't for the fact that, a few years ago, somebody thought to <u>scan the tax code</u> into computer language, we'd all still be in the dark about it. But now, thanks to deep-digging <u>Internet search programs</u>, the code is easily penetrated and its "secrets" are finally revealed for <u>anyone</u> to seek out. There is no longer any excuse— except laziness and cowardice— to being deaf, dumb, and blind about the income tax.

Maybe this is your wake-up call!

Remember that movie in which the main character, an enraged TV newsman, urged his viewers to go to their windows and yell out, *"I'm mad as hell and I'm not going to take it any more!"* ? Ring a bell ?

https://www.youtube.com/watch?v=ThB0uAbjhGY

Segment 5 – Falling Into the IRS Trap!

There are many surprises in store for you when you begin to discover the several ways and times over the years that the government has slyly and bit by bit contrived to circumvent the Constitution. The basic law of the land — the Constitution— lists 17 things which the federal government was empowered by the States to handle. Seventeen —that is all— like running the post office, coining money, determining correct weights and measures, and raising an army and navy.

You will look in vain for anything in the Constitution about Education, about TV signals, about Housing, about Central Banking, about Labor, about Medical Insurance. Virtually <u>everything</u> the federal government does today is derived from an <u>emanation</u>, an <u>extension</u>, a <u>figurative assumption</u> —however remote— either of one of the 17 items of responsibility listed in Section VIII of the Constitution, or from the <u>Welfare</u> or <u>Interstate Commerce</u> clauses.

The Great Crash of 1929, when the stock market plummeted to virtually nothing over a few days, opened the door to the Franklin Roosevelt administration in 1932. FDR was born to riches and grew up imbued with the "progressive" ideals of Woodrow Wilson, the architect of our World War I adventures. Faced with millions out of work, FDR moved to have his administration **"do something"** to create jobs, provide old-age pensions and other benefits for the populace. Sound familiar? **FDR called it the New Deal**, and it included the Social Security benefit package.

It was like giving candy to starving children. It was **"the right thing to do"** and government was the proper tool to do it with, according to FDR and his progressives. He was greatly popular, as Santa Claus always is.

The big problem for FDR was that there was nothing in the Constitution that permitted the federal government to concern itself with Social Welfare applicable to the 50 States. <u>There still isn't</u>. The Constitution does however allow the federal government to exercise municipal authority <u>within</u> the ("internal") boundaries of the District of Columbia and any U.S. territory (such as Puerto Rico and Guam), and to subject anyone <u>acting with its permission</u> to certain related duties and obligations. Popular understanding of these limits had faded over the early years of the 20th Century (in fact, that understanding was under constant assault by Liberal/Progressives over that whole period, extending even to today).

So FDR's Social Security program, and later the programs of federal Medicare and, arguably, Obamacare, were carefully written to properly confine themselves to those reachable by federal authority, and were only made <u>voluntary</u> for the populace within the external 50 States. Yes, you read that correctly: *voluntary*. But strenuous efforts have been made to convince the American public otherwise, and to trick people into "<u>volunteering</u>". There's actually nothing in the Social Security law that says that you and I <u>must</u> take part in that program. We can <u>elect</u> to participate if we want to. However, Congress has contrived over the years to make it very difficult for anyone to survive in society <u>without</u> giving the appearance of having "<u>volunteered</u>"

themselves into those programs. Try going without a Social Security number for about two minutes nowadays.

Since the "system" is designed to suck us into the tax swamp, it can be difficult to stop volunteering for it even when we know what's going on. But it's a do-able chore, and oh so nice when accomplished.

Tens of thousands have already disassociated themselves quite legally from the Personal and Business tax scheme, especially since about 2003, when these truths about the tax were finally fathomed and "began to gain public notice." Thousands began asking for all of their past withheld payroll tax money back —and receiving it!

The key to extricating yourself is knowing about those "terms of art" and then taking steps to align yourself with the law. It's not always an easy process because you are flying in the face of conventional practices and beliefs, especially when you confront the person or company who hires and pays you. You rarely will find these people sympathetic. Instead, they will almost inevitably hide behind their accountant's advice. That's the "My CPA makes me do it" excuse.

A major part of the scheme is the matter of the annual IRS Information trap:

At the end of each calendar year, the company or individual you work for reports to the IRS that you have been paid **"wages"** and that certain amounts of taxes were withheld from your pay, per your Form W-4 request. Your "employer" reports it all to the IRS under penalty of perjury, and his reports are then held as sworn testimony that you have been paid earnings subject to the income tax.

Forms <u>W-2</u>, <u>1099's</u>, <u>K-1's</u>, and <u>W-2G's</u> are called information returns. They are not the *final* word about your earnings but they become the basis of the IRS's tax collection operations.

If you then don't <u>own up to</u> —or rebut— these information return allegations on your annual tax return, the IRS comes looking for you with its full array of penalties and interest —especially if they deem you to be acting "frivolously" while attempting to extricate yourself from them.

The way out of the dilemma is to attach an affidavit to your annual tax return that corrects or rebuts the information that was falsely reported to the IRS. Your tax return acts to supersede the incorrect or inaccurate information about your earnings on W-2's and 1099's. Surprisingly, the IRS itself has whispered this solution (if you know where to look for it), and in tens of thousands of "educated" returns, has fully (and quietly) accepted them.

Certified Public Accountants, tax attorneys, outfits like H&R Block, and tax preparation software programs like TurboTax are all part of the multi-billion dollar <u>income tax industry</u>. Individuals have passed tests to earn their credentials, but 99.9% of their training deals entirely with the <u>practices</u>, <u>procedures</u>, and <u>allowable deductions</u>

concerning the payment of the tax to the government. <u>They are taught *nothing* about the terms of art in the tax code</u>! And they have no *incentive* to want to change their ways. In fact, IRS awards them brownie points for closely adhering to IRS dictates.

From personal experience, I know that you will receive quizzical looks from your CPA if you ask him/her about this —like you are out of your mind. You will likely be told, "Don't listen to that guy —he'll only get you into trouble."

But it is also true that once an "expert" learns these truths (and a growing number are learning them and spreading the word), they find that they can no longer complete tax forms for clients as they did before —not if they're true to their professional oaths.

Segment 6– Troubles with W-4 and W-9

The easiest way to avoid the tax system's traps is to become an independent contractor; i.e., work for yourself. Hire yourself. Be your own boss. In fact, this is good advice at any time, taxes or not. Create your own job —go into business for yourself. Just don't open your "lemonade stand" on federal government property.

Note that I didn't say to become **"self-employed"** because that too is a term of art. You can work for yourself and not be "self-employed." But if you operate your lemonade stand on federal property, then you do indeed fit the legal definition as "self-employed" and the taxman is entitled to a piece of your action.

Working for yourself eliminates the two troublesome enrollment forms, the W-4, and W-9. However, another IRS information form may come into play: the 1099-MISC. Those are issued by businesses for which you did some work, saying that you were paid a listed amount of "taxable income." But 1099s are much easier to deal with, and you even get the support of the IRS in doing so. All you need do is refer to the IRS instructions for those issuing 1099-MISC, 1099-INT, and 1099-DIV where it says, **"Use** (1099 forms) **only for reporting funds paid out from your trade or business."**

Well, of course, **"trade or business"** is a legal term, and now that you know that, it becomes easy to rebut an information form from someone purporting to be a **"trade or business"** contrary to fact. When your own enterprise is not a **"trade or business"** you are the only one with first-hand information about it.

The other problem form that IRS uses is the W-9, in spite of the fact that it is not an official form (has no OMB number on it) and IRS doesn't want anything to do with it after you fill it out. It is a strange sort of beast, but it does complicate things.

Reduced to its basics the W-9 asks for two things: the first is your tax identification number which in most cases is your social security number. The second is in two parts: you are asked to certify that you are not subject to withholding because of some income tax problem you may have previously been involved with. And you are asked to certify that you are a **"U.S. Person"**.

A **"U.S. Person"** is another of those pesky "terms of art." The typical uneducated response is, sure, I'm a **U.S. Person**, born right here in this State. So you quickly answer **"Yes"**. However, your "Yes" answer actually admits that you are among a special class of persons subject to particular provisions of the tax laws. In other words, **"U.S. Person"** does NOT simply mean **"American"**.

An irony about the W-9 is that it specifically instructs that the form is not to be returned to the IRS. Businesses, as well as banks and investment firms, are required to ask for tax I.D. numbers from enrollees, but there is nothing in the law that requires enrollees to complete the form. However, over the years the process has shifted from a properly permissive one to a mandatory one. Nowadays, if you refuse to complete the W-9 form, you will not be hired or be allowed to open a bank or investment account.

On the other hand, some bosses and some banks will permit you to expand the **"U.S. Person"** answer from a simple checkmark. After all, the form *does* remain in their hands. You may then write in wording to the effect that, No, you are not a "U.S. Person" as that term is defined in the tax code, but you were born in California, or Kentucky, or whatever the case may be. That will satisfy the bank's "need to be able to certify (for Homeland Security purposes) that **you are a citizen of your State**, and are not an alien.

While the W-4 and W-9 are troublesome, the most important form of all is the Form 1040, your tax return. You definitely need to file a United States tax return for any year in which anyone reports to the government that you have received earnings in excess of a stipulated minimum, the amount of which changes each year according to a formula. That is true whether you owe any tax or not— because the reporting to the government of payments to you also constitutes a declaration that those payments were received in connection with the conduct of taxable activities.

To be clear, you must also file a Form 1040 to report gains from taxable activities —if any— whether anyone else reports them or not —as long as they total the current exemption amount or more.

Nothing in the law requires use of the official Form 1040 for filing a return. Any sworn document containing the exact same information may be used. However, using the Form 1040 is the simplest way to go about it. Either way, filing a return requires you to swear under penalty of perjury that the information you've entered on the form is true, accurate, and complete to the best of your knowledge and belief. By law, then, the contents are accepted by the IRS as your sworn testimony, unless those worthies have first-hand knowledge that some entry or other is in error. Burden of proof for that falls on the government.

Who else but you can have first-hand knowledge of your earnings status?

You're at the IRS's not-so-tender mercies if you aren't aware of the "terms of art" and how to apply their legal meanings for your own benefit. However, armed with that and other procedural knowledge, you can properly regain your controlling position in respect to the federal <u>excise tax</u> on certain income.

You again are in control.

Having said that, I need to advise you specifically that you need to know much more about all of this than I have space to tell you here.

Segment 7– So What Do You Do Now?

I hope the previous six segments have made you aware of the central facts concerning the federal income tax. To make use of this new knowledge —to put <u>yourself</u> right with the tax code— requires that you do more self-educating on the subject. I have provided only the broad strokes here, but not all the specifics you need to have. It's not a simple subject —there is a lot more to know and understand.

Don't look to your CPA or tax preparer for help. All most all of those people are well-meaning, but totally ignorant of any of this. They are part of the problem.

There is no doubt that your life will be less complicated if you **"go with the flow"** just as you have been doing. "Go along to get along", is the saying. However, "going along" in this case means that you cooperate with what amounts to outright thievery by continuing to volunteer your hard-earned money to the extortion process of the IRS. Maybe you do not mind doing that, but many *do* mind.

There is also no doubt that the IRS and others in the Department of Treasury know full well that the income tax is an excise tax, and that they knowingly collude to operate it as a direct tax on your income instead. They mainly accomplished that with the use of terms of art by deliberately remaining silent about them.

Their silence is supplemented by a deliberate program of instilling fear of prosecution and penalties, and by deliberately fudging the legalities surrounding their use of levies and liens. This is another part of the story I have not covered here.

Even if your total earnings and deductions and exemptions already put you into the zero tax category, and you're not paying any tax at all, it's empowering to know about the terms of art and how they serve to make dupes out of all those who *do* pay taxes not actually owed. You can spread the word and help boost people's knowledge of the importance of the Constitution to our personal freedom.

As a bonus, in the process you will also learn similar vital truths about capital gains taxes and federal estate transfer taxes —because the matter of terms of art applies to them too. It's an allied subject, worthy of attention by itself.

If you dismiss what you've read here, and shrug it off as nonsense, then there is little hope for you. You live to be taken advantage of. Stay out of poker games...

On the other hand, if you have some backbone and want to stop the IRS from extorting your earning from you, then you need to learn how to swing behind you the weight of law. This is a very comfortable position to be in!

The really good news is that the IRS finally does accede to the law, as they must. They just hope that the general public doesn't find out what's really going on, because the wheels will then come off the tax goodies cart. Americans will regain their freedom to earn, and to keep what they do earn. Because I've only covered the surface of the subject here, you need to read the "bible" of it all, a book entitled ***Cracking the Code—the Fascinating Truth About Taxation in America,*** in its 15th printing as of this is writing. Authored by Peter E. Hendrickson. It's being promulgated by person to person, word of mouth, and it is an eye-opener.

Hendrickson's book is available at **www.losthorizons.com**. Read and re-read it until you become totally conversant with the entire subject. There is *also* a wealth of information on that website, including photocopies of some 1,000 checks and documents showing specifically and actually how States and the IRS have acceded to the demands for the full return of some $12 Million dollars in taxes previously paid due to ignorance of the truths and facts underlying the U.S. income tax.

What do you have to lose?

Segment 8—Why It's Important...

The purpose of this follow-up segment is to shine further light on what's been presented to you today.

I became interested in all of this taxation stuff back in 1977 when I was studying for my <u>Chartered Financial Consultant</u> designation from American College in Bryn Mawr, Pennsylvania. One of the 13 courses dealt with the "practical aspects" of the federal income tax. It was presented in textbooks having the imprimatur of the Internal Revenue Service. In other words, I learned about taxes from the IRS standpoint —which is the (wrongly, as you know now) assumption that whatever you earn or are paid, except for allowable deductions, is reportable and taxable to boot. This is all that the IRS cares about.

The emphasis for tax practitioners was on which <u>deductions and exemptions</u> are proper and allowable and which forms are to be completed at what time. There was nothing whatever in there about how to determine whether personal and business earnings are taxable in the first place or not. There was nothing about the use of Terms of Art in the code (IRC).

In those days, we were dealing with the most recent (1954) version of the tax code. As I studied the material I noticed some odd things that called for further answers. One of the biggies for me was why the system requires tax returns to be signed and submitted to IRS under penalty of perjury, with the information entered open to many government agencies to be used against you for whatever purpose they might have. What happened to the Fifth Amendment protection against self incrimination?

No answer anywhere.

Another was some weird wording I kept running into. As, for instance, where a code section says something like, "All persons required under this title to do such and such..." That indicated to me logically that there must then be some people who are NOT required to do such and such under this title. What about them?

No answer anywhere.

Those were the days before the entire tax code was scanned into computer language accessible to anyone with a computer. Before then, all research into the code had to be done manually, plowing through literally millions of words in the code with only a bare-bones index to help out. It was a timeconsuming, daunting task. Who had the time and patience for that sort of thing? I certainly did not.

So I went a long time without finding any substantial answers. Then, in 2006, I stumbled onto **Peter Hendrickson's book. Wow!** Here was a scholarly guy who spent many months on his computer, digging deeply into all aspects of the tax code, checking out each and every cross-reference (**scores of those!**) and the underlying the **Statutes at Large** that the code is based upon. I speed-read his book cover to cover in a couple of hours, and then read it again slowly, underlining passages, and writing notes in the margins. At the time, the book was in its fourth printing. It's now in its 15th printing!

At last I had the answers I had looked for all those years. Now I understood. And now I could tell others about **"my" find**. The answers, in *"Cracking the Code..."* also led me to realizations about many other financial matters in which the federal government is an **often corrupt and heavy handed player**.

It is now clear to me that the federal government has become the **King Kong gorilla in the room**, not at all what the Founding Fathers intended to occur, in the Declaration of Independence and the Constitution. Americans today have lost many of the freedoms guaranteed by the Constitution. Sadly, most of them have become conditioned to their status —too readily believing that government is the fundamental source of help, and good in their lives.

<u>This is why</u> this info is important. I am personally adamant not to play tax patsy to the federal government, nor can I remain quiet about it all, with my clients and friends.

Back before World War II, very few paid the income tax, or even knew that it existed. There were no payroll taxes, no withholdings. What you earned is what you got to keep. Doctors made house calls. I remember gasoline at 14 cents a gallon.

However, FDR needed money to finance World War II. The government began <u>begging</u> the public to <u>volunteer</u> to buy war bonds regularly. I can remember <u>Donald Duck ads</u> urging people to buy war bonds and help fight Hitler and Tojo. To make volunteering easier, the pay-as-you-go method first seen in Lincoln's day was re-introduced, wherein individuals authorized certain amounts of money to be withheld from their paychecks for the purchase of war bonds, and to pay the few cents required for enrollees in FDR's social security program.

You paid $18.75 for a bond, and after 10 years, you cashed it in for $25.00, for an gain of $6.25. America responded with great enthusiasm throughout the war time. It was the patriotic thing to do.

After the war —probably in the late 40's— it occurred to some bright lights in government that since the people responded so well to the <u>withholding idea</u>, why not continue to keep the money ball rolling. And so it was. Gradually, requesting withholding funds for paying the tax "as you go" became the unquestioned routine. Now it is almost universally considered mandatory.

But now you know better…..

Segment 9 – A Question about Information Returns

One of my correspondents asks for a fuller explanation of why <u>Forms W-2 and 1099</u> are issued and why they can create an <u>IRS trap</u> for her. Let's start by also showing clearly, by example, how ignorance of <u>Terms of Art</u> traps you into the income tax system. Here is an important one —in boldface and underlined. <u>Section 6041</u> is cited as the authority in the tax code that requires businesses to send earnings information to the IRS.

26 USC Section 6041. <u>Information at source</u>

(a) Payments of $600 or more

All **persons** engaged in a **trade or business** and making payment in the course of such **trade or business** to another **person**, of rent, salaries, **wages**, premiums, annuities, compensations, remunerations, emoluments, or other fixed or determinable **gains, profits and income** (other than payments to which Section 6042(a)(1), 6044(a)(1), 6047(e), or 6049(a) applies, and other than payments with respect to which a statement is required under the authority of Section 6042(a)(2), 6044(a)(2), or 6045), of $600 or more in any taxable year, or, in the case of such payments made by the **United States**, the officers or **employees** of the **United States** having information as to such payments and required to make returns in regard thereto by the regulations hereinafter provided for, shall render a true and accurate return to the Secretary, under such regulations and in such form and manner and to such extent as may be prescribed by the Secretary, setting forth the amount of such **gains, profits, and income**, and the name and address of the recipient of such payment.

Whew! First of all, you see here an example of the verbosity of the tax code. That's all just one sentence!

Second of all, while the bold-faced and underlined Terms here alert you that those terms have special meanings, they are not presented to the public in this way in the code. They are not set in bold face, as I have done for you here, so they appear as ordinary words. Unless they and their special definitions are known and recognized, they will mislead you.

It's important to note also that the governing phrase in that section is "All persons engaged in a trade or business...." Two Terms of Art are contained in there. The governing one is "trade or business." This Term is defined in the code to mean: "the conduct of the affairs of a public office." A public office is an officially designated entity connected to an element of the federal government.

Thus, anyone educated in the tax code and its terms of art knows immediately that the entire Section 6041 does not apply if the subject enterprise is NOT a "trade or business," no matter how many regulations the Secretary may attach to it. The code section could fill several pages (as some do) and none of it applies unless a **"trade or business"** is involved.

Another Term of Art in there is **"Persons"**. Its definition also is limiting and refers either to certain individuals or to business entities which equate to a **"trade or business."**

So, unless your boss's enterprise falls into that "trade or business" category, he/she should not be reporting your earnings as "self-employment income" or "non-employee compensation," assuming they amount to $600 or more.

When the IRS receives a false information return (the great majority of them!) from a business entity, the IRS treats it as positive evidence of taxable earnings, because when submitting those forms, business owners falsely "swear under penalty of perjury" that their enterprise is a "trade or business" that has paid taxable income to the people named. If that's you, you then need either to pay the tax on the amounts entered on the W-2 or 1099 (which is what you've been doing), or rebut the information given.

Rebutting the incorrect information must be done in such a way that you don't end up compounding the original problem. You're just getting started here...

The reader should note that the website **www.losthorizons.com** features more than 1,000 photocopied examples of corrected tax returns and the resultant rebate checks from IRS and State governments totaling several millions of dollars. (See the page at **www.losthorizons.com/BulletinBoard.htm**) These are known (by IRS admission!) to be only a small fraction of the tens of thousands of former "taxpayers" who now file "educated" annual returns that show, quite legitimately, that no taxable income has been earned and therefore no tax is due. Indeed, if the reader requires proof of the pudding, so to speak, there it is!

Segment X – What About Capital Gains?

Q. In Segment VII, you mentioned capital gains but didn't go into it at all. If I sell some stocks or other properties and make a profit, isn't that taxable?

Just like anything else involving the federal tax code, the matter of <u>Terms of Art</u> is a determining factor of the subject of capital gains, just as for the earnings you make from your work. I had intended to cover the subject of capital gains in a separate paper, but since you ask about it here, I'll do that now.

The IRS and the income tax industry would have you believe that if you have a property of some sort —whether it's real estate or not— and sell it at a profit, you must pay a tax on the gain involved. If you sell that property at a loss, then you must consider whether it's a <u>short-term loss</u> or a <u>long-term loss</u> to determine how the loss may be deducted from earnings. Etc. Etc. CPA's love it, because then they can show off how knowledgeable they are about tax deductions.

In actuality, the first thing to be determined is whether the property involved is <u>subject to the capital gains law in the</u>

first place. Chances are good that the capital gains provision in the tax code does not apply to your stock shares because they are <u>outside</u> the purview of the tax code. Selling those for a gain or loss is <u>outside</u> the Federal reach.

As you consider this, you must always remember that the Constitution prohibits any <u>direct tax</u> unless it is apportioned by population through the external 50 States. <u>Indirect taxes</u> are allowed, as an impost, a duty, or an excise. However, these types of taxes can only apply to things <u>having</u> a direct nexus to the federal government.

There are several sections of the tax code that deal with various aspects of capital gains. Each of them includes <u>Terms of Art</u> limiting the things to which the sections apply to those connected with the federal government in one way or another. The general rules for determining capital gains are to be found in <u>Section 1222</u> of the code. So, that's the first place to look.

Here we see that capital gains concern the "sale or exchange of a **capital asset**." Therefore, unless what is sold or exchanged is a <u>capital asset</u> as defined in the tax code, the gain or loss is not subject to <u>capital gain</u> levies.

So next we must check the definition for **"capital asset"** to see if your stock shares fit the bill. We find the definition in <u>Section 1221(a)</u>. Its wording includes other terms of art that we must also check out.

Here is how it reads:

"For purposes of this subtitle [income tax], the term **"capital asset"** means property held by the taxpayer (whether or not connected with his <u>trade or business</u>), but does not include [my emphasis] the following:

> (1) stock in trade of the **taxpayer** or other property of a kind which would properly be included in the inventory of the **taxpayer**…or property held by the **taxpayer** primarily for sale to customers in the ordinary course of his **trade or business**.

> (2) property, used in his **trade or business**, of a character which is subject to the allowance for depreciation provided in Section 167, or real property used in his **trade or business**.

The term **"trade or business"** is of particular distinction in any reference to capital gains. But there's another term that takes <u>precedence</u>: **"taxpayer"**.

"We must ask ourselves why the code writers thought it necessary to repeat the term **"taxpayer"** four times in the section defining a **capital asset**. **"Taxpayer"** is defined in <u>Section 7701(a)(14)</u> as "<u>any **person** subject to any internal revenue tax</u>." "Person" is also a Term of Art referring to individuals or businesses involved in a "<u>Trade or Business</u>".

Using a bit of logic, we can conclude that if there are "**taxpayers**" there must *also* be "non-**taxpayers**." In other words, the code sections concerning capital gains are for **taxpayers** only. This would be any entity with earnings derived from some sort of connection to the federal government. If you are one of those, then the other terms of art in there come into play.

When you read Section 1221 in its entirety, you can become bamboozled by its verbosity, cross references, and double negatives. It's a difficult read because the tax code writers didn't much give a damn if what they wrote is immediately comprehensible. Their primary chore is not clarity, but to keep the tax law Constitutional —which it is. However, their meaning becomes clear only when you apply the tax code's definitions of the terms of art.

What Section 1221 amounts to is this: If you are not a **taxpayer**, then a property such as stock or real estate or article of personal ownership is not a **capital asset** and therefore not subject to any federal taxation.

Just to be clear about the meaning of **"taxpayer"** in the tax code, it refers to anyone who is obligated for an internal revenue tax, such as "income" taxes and certain other specific excises. You might pay any number and amount of other types of taxes, and still not be a "taxpayer" to whom a capital gains levy applies. I couldn't find a Supreme Court ruling about it, but a federal court's ruling in Montana in 1922 still stands and serves to further clarify the term for us:

> **"The revenue laws are a code or system in regulation of tax assessment and collection. They relate to taxpayers, and not to non-taxpayers. The latter are without their scope. No procedure is prescribed for**

non-taxpayers, and no attempt is made to annul any of their rights and remedies in due course of law. <u>With them Congress does not assume to deal</u>, and they are neither of the subject nor of the object of the revenue laws...."

>Long v. Rasmussen, Collector of Internal Revenue, et al.
>--District Court, D. Montana (281 F. 236 [1922])

The U.S. <u>Internal</u> Revenue is the Revenue of the <u>Internal</u> U.S.
i.e.,
The District of Columbia and its U.S. Territories which are <u>Internal</u> to the U.S.A.

<u>A Caveat</u>:

The reader of the foregoing pages should understand that none of what I have presented here is a protest of the income tax itself. Anyone who has <u>taxable income</u> is obliged by law to report it and pay whatever tax is due on it, and that certainly should be done. My sole purpose is to alert the reader to the fact that <u>the tax</u>, as it is written and practiced, <u>is widely misconstrued</u>, and that these widespread misunderstandings are knowingly encouraged by the federal government, the President, and the Congress, and especially encouraged by the IRS in order to induce payment of taxes <u>not actually owed</u>. This is the shameful truth about the federal income tax.

Misunderstanding The Internal Revenue Code Costs Americans About A Trillion Dollars Every Year

Understanding It Costs Only $29.95

http://www.losthorizons.com/Cracking_the_Code.htm

"You Know Something is Wrong When…..An American Affidavit of Probable Cause"

http://tinyurl.com/hh2ug3u

You Know Something is Wrong When.....
An American Affidavit of Probable Cause

https://www.createspace.com/4390079

Password = *password*

Miscellaneous Writings
featuring Anna von Reitz

https://www.createspace.com/700022

Password = *password*

"As It Is The Truth"
by Judge Anna von Reitz

https://www.createspace.com/6470330

Password = *password*

Disclosure 101
What You Need To Know

https://www.createspace.com/4870915

Password = *password*

Rogue Sabre Special Ops
by Task-Force-Sheepdog

https://www.createspace.com/7053961

Password = *password*

Made in the USA
Las Vegas, NV
07 June 2022